MW01277212

essence of LINEN

Hilary Mandleberg

essence of LINEN

RYLAND
PETERS
& SMALL

London New York

First published in the United States in 2001
by Ryland Peters & Small, Inc.
519 Broadway, 5th Floor
New York NY10012
www.rylandpeters.com

10 9 8 7 6 5 4 3 2 1

Text, design, and photographs
© Ryland Peters & Small 2001

Jacket picture credits:
Front flap, spine and main jacket image by Polly Wreford
Front inset image by James Merrell
Back flap and back jacket image by David Loftus

Printed and bound in China

Library of Congress Cataloging-in-Publication Data

Mandleberg, Hilary.
   Essence of linen / Hilary Mandleberg.
     p. cm. -- (Essence books)
   ISBN 1-84172-177-8
   1. Textile fabrics in interior decoration. 2. Linen. I. Title. II. Series.

NK2115.5.F3 M36 2001
747'.9 --dc21   2001031622

contents

Timeless — **6**

A Gordian Knot — 10

Fit for the Gods — 14

Textures & Shades — **16**

Spinning Yarn — 18

Pretty in Pink — 20

Live — **24**

Eclectic Style — 26

In from the Cold — 30

Eat — **34**

Laundering Linen — 36

Tea for Two — 42

Manners Maketh Man — 44

Sleep — **46**

Sleeping Beauty — 48

Bathe — **54**

Wet & Wild — 56

Credits — 62

timeless

Not a beautiful lock of hair, but some hackled flax waiting to be spun. Linen manufacture has hardly changed over the centuries. The product is as dependable as ever.

Everyone knows the ancient Egyptians used linen—as many as 450 square yards at one time—for wrapping up their mummies. But ten-thousand-year-old layers of the fabric, found on a burial couch in Gordion in Asia Minor, show it has an even older pedigree.

A GORDIAN KNOT

Once linen was worn by rich and poor alike, but when modern synthetics took the hard work out of fabric care, it seemed to fall from favor. Happily, people have now come to appreciate the esthetic, spiritual, and ecological advantages of this truly great fabric.

Linen is made from the stem of flax, a plant that grows everywhere the climate is temperate and moist. In modern times, central Europe, as well as Ireland and the United States, have all enjoyed thriving linen industries that declined only when cheaper cotton came on the scene. Linen's long journey from flax field to cloth is marked by the soaking of the stems ("retting"), crushing and beating ("scutching"), and combing or "hackling."

Clothes designers adore linen. It is resilient, cool, hardwearing, absorbent, and, as it's static-free, it drapes well. No wonder it has hardly ever been out of fashion. In ancient times, garments made of white linen were prized as symbols of purity and were used by

FIT FOR THE GODS

Egyptians and, later, Jews, for their religious ceremonies. Today, linen is for every day. From the finest sheers to heavy, close weaves, linen suits all styles and seasons. The only fabric to improve with washing, crease-resistant treatments now make linen even better.

textures & shades

Even after years of use, a rough old linen grain sack can still charm its way into a modern home, for part of linen's enduring appeal lies in its varied textures. After combing, the flax is spun. Wet spinning softens the gums in the fibers and produces

SPINNING YARN

fine, regular yarn used for clothing. Dry spinning gives the heavier yarn needed for canvas, upholstery fabrics, and many other household textiles. A handkerchief or shirt might be a plain weave, while a firm, close, twill weave is used for curtains or suiting.

Our current love affair with all things natural means that unbleached linen's brownish color and the creamy white of bleached linen have found new favor. But color rules, too, and has for centuries. Some linens found in the Egyptian tombs were dyed using

PRETTY IN PINK

vegetable dyes such as indigo, madder, and saffron. Today, we have a huge choice of long-lasting synthetic dyes at our disposal, and linen just soaks them up. Shocking pink linen slacks and linen slippers are fine examples of what modern dye techniques can do.

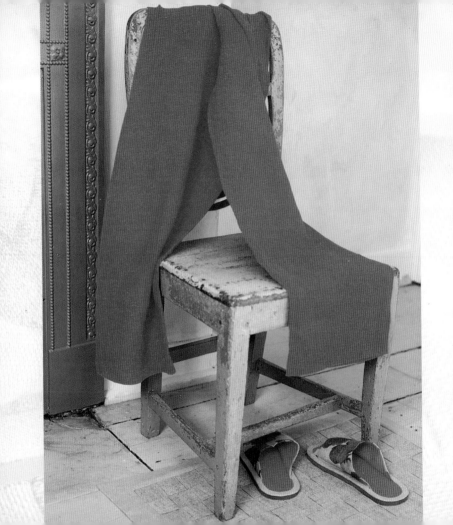

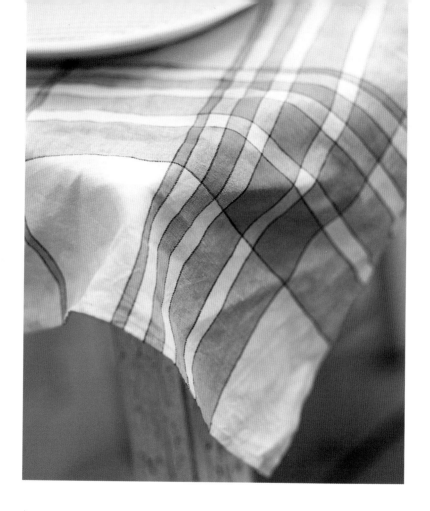

textures & shades

A simple green and cream linen cloth conjures up the freshness of spring, while rough brown linen placemats bring a hint of the Orient to the table.

live

Linen is the Jekyll and Hyde of the textile world. It's just as much at home in the shape of fine woven fabrics and lace as it is in sacking and twine. Hence its ability to blend easily with a multitude of decorating styles, from rustic simplicity to urban

ECLECTIC STYLE

chic, and everything in between. A French provincial living room full of stone and antiques is saved from being cold and uninviting, thanks to an authentic, battered old park bench, a quirky log lamp, and a huge linen cloth spread casually over the table.

Snuggle up in front of a fire with a good book—linen-bound of course—and a supply of logs from a linen bag to keep you warm through the winter.

Once, the wealthy would just as soon have gone out in the street naked as decorate their living room with linen. Linen was what you used to cover up your fine silk and damask furniture and protect it from the sun when it was not in use. Now linen's virtues

IN FROM THE COLD

are on show in the most tasteful of homes. Neutral color schemes are pepped up by the varied textures of linen, and you can always add leather, wood, and woven cane to the equation. And as for those linen throws— of course, they're today's must-haves.

eat

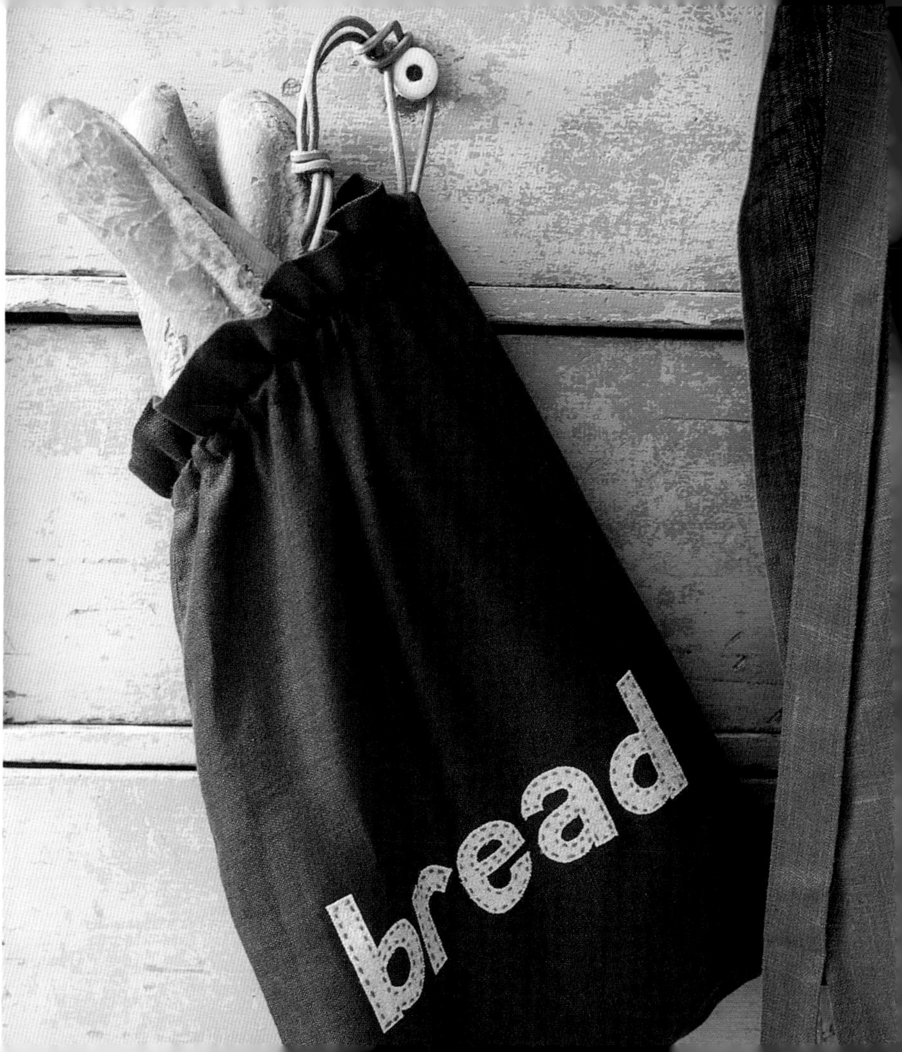
bread

Linen is robust enough to withstand the toughest laundry treatments and the highest temperatures, so it's ideal for messy napkins and tablecloths. By some miracle, every time it's washed, a subtle molecular change takes place around each fiber, so the fabric comes

LAUNDERING LINEN

up looking like new. Iron it while it's damp, add spray starch if you choose, and you'll have table linen that's fit for kings and princes to dine from. And if laundering isn't your scene, then why not just store your crunchy sticks of bread in a funky linen bag?

Even if you live in the urban jungle, you can still bring a touch of the country into your life. Take time to make your own jelly and jam, then seal them in a traditional way with circles of waxed paper, and cover them with natural linen tied with string. Serve with tea, on a jolly linen patchwork napkin with milk in a blue china pitcher. With a plateful of sandwiches and slices of cake on the side, could you ask for more?

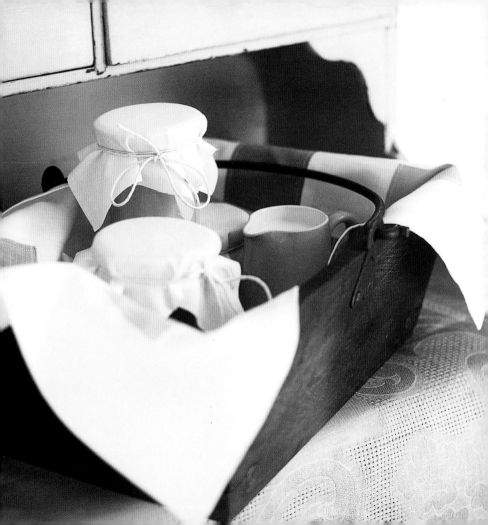

Embroidery and linen—a combination
that has withstood the test of time,
for what else is the Bayeux Tapestry but
a linen strip embroidered in wool? You
may not have the time or inclination to

embroider bouquets, initials, or your coat-of-arms on linen napkins, so why not cheat? Scour antique flea markets and you're bound to find examples you'll be proud to display on the table.

TEA FOR TWO

Fine bone china, silver spoons,
and embroidered linen napkins—
a nostalgic teatime treat.

The table is laid with crisp linen at an elegant wedding breakfast. For centuries, the best linen has always been reserved for formal occasions. Households of note would have table linens of the finest figured damask that would be handed down through

MANNERS MAKETH MAN

generations. Patterns included heraldic crests, mottoes, dates—even perhaps the name or initials of the person who commissioned the cloth. But damask was only for the wealthy. It was costly to produce and required an army of servants to keep it looking like new.

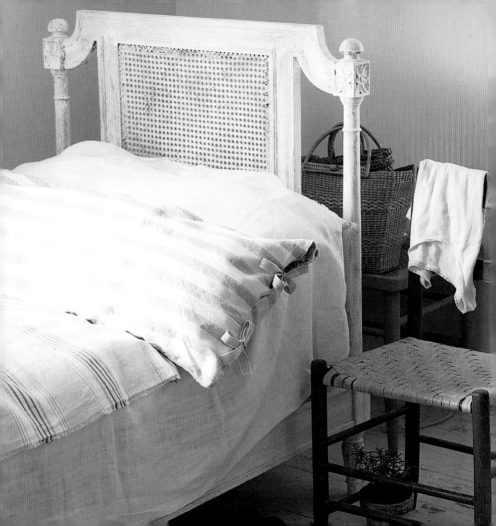

sleep

Linen sheets are a far cry from easy-care cottons and synthetic blends. They need a lot of work to iron them smooth, but people who have slept between fine linen sheets swear that they would never sleep on anything else. There's something blissful and

SLEEPING BEAUTY

self-indulgent about the feel of linen next to the skin. The structure of the fiber makes it cool in summer, yet warm and cozy in winter. And you can choose from severe linens enlivened only by a contrasting stripe, or linens edged in lace, ribbon, bows, and tucks.

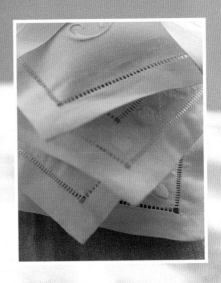

Heavy white embroidery and white lace inserts on white bedlinen are classics, reminiscent of the icing on a wedding cake. For extra bedtime bliss and to help you sleep, scent your bedroom with lavender-filled linen pillows.

The bedroom is somewhere we need to feel secure, and its textiles say a lot about the concerns of a particular society. In some of the Greek islands, bed tents suspended from a hook in the ceiling and made of panels of striking, multicolored embroidered linen announced to the world the power of the family that owned them. In the nineteenth century, many people were obsessed with cleanliness. Only crisp white linen sheets and austere iron bedsteads gave them the feeling that their bedrooms were germfree. The sternness of this look is back in vogue, but now it appears soft and forgiving in contrast to the cool asceticism of modern-day minimalism.

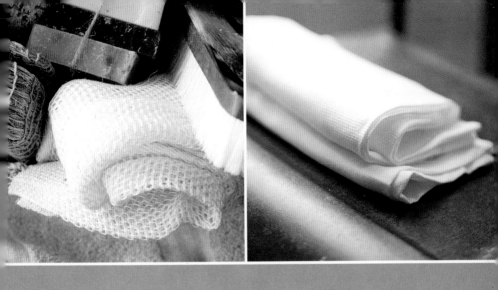

bathe

Linen and water go well together. It's stronger when it's wet, so it is the fiber of choice for ships' sails, fishing nets, and firemen's hoses. And it looks good in the bathroom, too, whether your taste is for the faded grandeur of antique gilded mirrors, old brass

WET & WILD

faucets and rolltop bathtubs, the modern thrills of a minimal bathroom kitted out in gleaming chrome and polished stone, or the homey warmth of wood, wicker, and handmade soap. So choose a loosely woven natural linen washcloth and start scrubbing!

You couldn't find a thirstier fabric if you tried. You may love the soft feel of a fluffy cotton towel, but for absorbency, nothing beats linen, so choose it for the finest face and guest towels. Many of them are made in a specially developed weave—known as honeycomb weave or huckaback. The

loose interlacing of the linen threads gives the finished fabric even greater absorbency. Many of the top hotels offer linen bath towels and robes. You, too, can indulge in the same luxury, but at home.

architects and designers featured in this book

Key: **a**=above, **b**=below, **l**=left, **r**=right, **t**=telephone, **f**=fax, **ph**=photographer

Annie's Vintage Costume
10 Camden Passage
London N1 8ED, UK
t. +44 (0)20 7359 0796
Pages 4–5, 6, 7 l

Aria
133 & 295–6 Upper Street
London N1 2TU, UK
t. +44 (0)20 7704
1999/72261021
f. +44 (0)20 7704 6333
www.aria-shop.co.uk
Pages 52–53

Claire Bataille & Paul ibens Design NV
Architects
Vekestraat 13 Bus 14
2000 Antwerpen, Belgium
t. +32 3231 3593
f. +32 3213 8639
Page 33

Cologne & Cotton
88 Marylebone High Street
London W1M 3DE, UK
t. +44 (0)20 7486 0595
Pages 50–51

De Le Cuona Textile and Home
Collection
Head Office:
9–10 Osbourne Mews
Windsor SL4 3DE, UK
email. bernie@softech.co.uk
www.delecuona.co.uk
Pages 25 l, 54, 55 l

B. Davis
t. 607 264 3673
Interior design; antique hand-dyed
linen, wool, silk textiles by yard,
home furnishings and clothing to
order.
Page 46

The Irish Linen Guild
5c The Square
Hillsborough
BT26 6AG
Northern Ireland, UK

Rob Merrett
t./f. +44 (0)20 7700 3269
Home accessories to order.
Pages 17 r, 2 l, 25 r, 28–29, 36,
38–39

Roger Oates Design
Shop & Showroom:
1 Munro Terrace, Cheyne Walk
London SW10 0DL, UK
Studio Shop:
The Long Barn
Eastnor, Ledbury
Herefordshire, HR8 1EL, UK
Mail-order catalog:
t. +44 (0)1531 631 611

useful addresses for where to buy linen

Rugs and runners.
Pages 1, 18, 24, 32 **bl**

Reed Creative Services Ltd
151a Sydney Street
London SW3 6NT, UK
t. +44 (0)20 7565 0066
f. +44 (0)20 7565 0067
Page 30

Shaker
72–73 Marylebone High Street
London W1V 5JW, UK
t. +44 (0)20 7935 9461
f. +44 (0)20 7935 4157
email. shaker@shaker.co.uk
www.shaker.co.uk
Page 60

ABC Carpet & Home Co., Inc.
881 & 888 Broadway
New York NY 10003
t. 212 473 3000
f. 212 420 1808
www.abchome.com

Bed Bath & Beyond
620 Ave of the Americas
New York NY 10011
t. 212 255 3550
www.bedbath.com

The Terence Conran Shop
407 East 59th Street
New York NY 10022
t. 212 755 9079
f. 212 888 3008
www.conran.com

Crate & Barrel
650 Madison Ave.
New York NY 10021
t. 212 308 0011

Nicole Fahri
10 East 60th Street
New York NY 10022
t. 212 421 7720

Pottery Barn
600 Broadway
New York NY 10012
t. 212 219 2420
127 E. 59th Street
New York NY 10022
t. 917 369 0050

Ralph Lauren
867 Madison Ave
New York NY 10021
t. 212 606 2100

credits 63

picture credits

Endpapers ph Polly Wreford

1 ph Andrew Wood/Roger Oates & Fay Morgan's house in Eastnor; **2 ph** Alan Williams/Toia Saibene's apartment in Milan;
3 ph Polly Wreford; **4–5, 6 & 7 l ph** Polly Wreford/Linda Garman's home in London, vintage linens from Annie's Vintage
Costume; **7 r ph** James Merrell; **8 ph** Polly Wreford; **9, 11 & 12–13 ph** David Loftus; **15 & 16 ph** Polly Wreford/Linda
Garman's home in London; **17 l ph** James Merrell; **17 r ph** Polly Wreford/Linda Garman's home in London, slippers and
rug by Rob Merrett; **18 ph** Andrew Wood/Roger Oates & Fay Morgan's house in Eastnor; **20 ph** Polly Wreford; **21 ph**
Polly Wreford/Linda Garman's home in London, slippers and rug by Rob Merrett; **22 ph** James Merrell; **23 ph** Tom
Leighton; **24 ph** Andrew Wood/Roger Oates & Fay Morgan's house in Eastnor; **25 l ph** Andrew Wood/Bernie de le Cuona's
house in Windsor; **25 r ph** Polly Wreford/book covers by Rob Merrett; **26 ph** Simon Upton/Maison d'Hôte; **28–29 ph**
Polly Wreford/Linda Garman's home in London, book covers and log carrier by Rob Merrett; **30 ph** Tom Leighton/Keith
Varty & Alan Cleaver's apartment in London designed by Jonathan Reed; **32 al & ar ph** James Merrell; **32 bl ph** Andrew
Wood/Roger Oates & Fay Morgan's house in Eastnor; **32 br ph** James Merrell/Janie Jackson stylist/designer; **33 ph**
Andrew Wood/a house near Antwerp designed by Claire Bataille & Paul ibens; **34 ph** Henry Bourne; **35 l ph** David Loftus;
35 r ph James Merrell; **36 ph** Polly Wreford/Linda Garman's home in London, bread bag by Rob Merrett; **38–39 ph** Polly
Wreford/Linda Garman's home in London, patchwork tablecloth by Rob Merrett; **40–43 ph** David Loftus; **45 ph** Polly
Wreford; **46 ph** James Merrell/Barbara Davis' house in upstate New York; **47 & 48 ph** James Merrell; **50–51 ph** Polly
Wreford/Linda Garman's home in London, bed linen from Cologne & Cotton; **51 inset ph** Polly Wreford; **52–53 ph**
Polly Wreford/Linda Garman's home in London, pure linen pyjamas from Aria; **54 & 55 l ph** Andrew Wood/Bernie de le
Cuona's house in Windsor; **55 r ph** Tom Leighton; **56 & 58–59 ph** Polly Wreford/Linda Garman's home in London; **60 ph**
Andrew Wood/Linen bathrobe by Shaker; **61 ph** Polly Wreford/Linda Garman's home in London.

The author and publisher would also like to thank all those whose homes or work are featured in this book.